Meetup@Blackrock

a meetup series memoir

"It's a mixed up, meetup, match me up world!"

By

Jethro atmeetupmemoirs

Sherry Craven

Respect414All Productions / Publishing

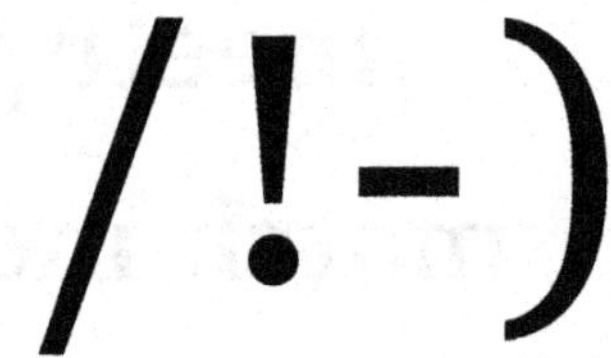

Copyright

Meetup@Blackrock
a
Respect414All Production / Publication
in association with
KDP Publishing a division of Amazon.com
©2017/!-)Sherry Craven/!-)Jethro
Cover Photo by: R414A Media Productions

ISBN: 978-1-7353642-1-6

Respect414All Productions / Publications
41723 Van Born Rd.
Belleville, MI 48111

Digitally / electronically / physically produced and published in the
United States of America

Jethro atmeetupmemoirs

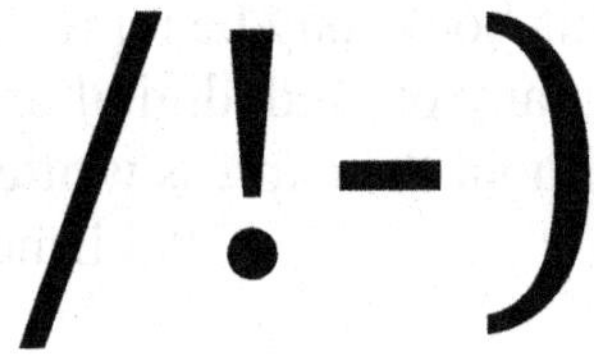

Dedication

All Meetup Series Memoirs are sincerely dedicated to Jeannine!!

"I'll do whatever you guys want..."

The wills that surround you can clearly hear... through the words you speak, in your tone of voice it's clear... you'll surrender your will to the one who voices her pleasure... simply thrilling to bring bodies, minds and spirits together...

Your gift to each one... indeed... virtually... all who show up in need, is to give them each, one by one, some of your time and interest in, where they may have been and what they may have done...

Nothing more, nothing less, than exactly what one needs... to find hope for the future and absolutely believe...

She matters to you and that you cannot wait for another... chance to get back together and possibly discover more fascinating facts about her, her life and her loves...

But for now, it's a warm and most sincere hug...

Before you ask... just to confirm...

"I'll see you next month?"

Smile and turn...

Then quickly check back, looking deeply into her eyes for a sign she felt genuinely welcomed and had a good time!!!

/!-)

Jethro atmeetupmemoirs

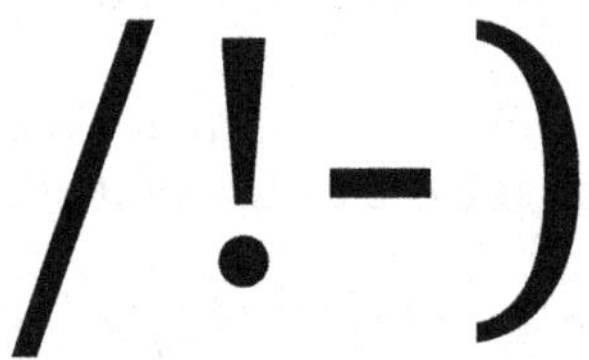

Meetup@Blackrock

/!-) Sounds like an old time western book title! /!-)

/!-) I may have to employ it... /!-)

One step over the threshold, opened a world of possibilities that put me literally, directly in her path.

October 14, 2016 must have been the date destiny had planned.

When she sat down next to me at the Meetup at Hayden's I tried to keep an open mind that what I had seen in her eyes at Black Rock wasn't true.

Surely, not even the "universe", could deliver me the exact circumstance I'd been waiting for in the form of a single, (meaning "one", not "available"), person that could lead me in the direction, I needed to go...

Jethro atmeetupmemoirs

Tested, I chose to seize the opportunity destiny had provided by acknowledging the connections that had to take place for us to be in the same place and time.

Recognition of the numerous possibilities, future interactions with her might bring, gave me faith that through acknowledgement of the destiny involved, I could place the details of that destiny in its and her hands.

It was a long 24 hours or so between the time I rounded the front corner of Hayden's out of her sight, hyper aware, for the first time in a very long time that my fate was in someone's hands other than my own and the time I turned my phone on to discover her text telling me that she had entered my dues and I was all set on her Meetup site.

Prone to imaginative interpretation of the written word, I spent the rest of that evening "spinning" the words, "it was nice meeting you and look forward to seeing you again", which may or may not have been intended to be as infused with meaning as my spirit hoped and was joyfully spinning into another test of fate.

Knowing myself well enough to know I would not be happy if I passed up the opportunity to play, I responded to my interpretation of her words by volleying back with an implication of my own desire to play the next day.

/!-) How went the bowling, Grasshopper? Did your skill allow you to overcome the challenge of your opponents? "It went well, 5 of us went; was fun; thanks for asking." ;)

/!-) Is there a meetup this weekend? /!-)

"There is; we're going to meetup @ Blake's Apple Orchard for the Haunted Hay Ride, Saturday." ;)

/!-) During the day?

/!-) Not seeing the fun in that unless we're all blindfolded!/!-)

"Lol" "We're meeting at the ticket booth at 6:45p.m.; haunted hayrides aren't much fun during the day!!" ;)

"Think blindfolded can be fun sometimes though!!" ;)[][][][]

(After I was able to catch my breath, I responded...)

/!-) This phone won't display emoji's, so I'll just have to use my imagination to interpret what they were... /!-)

"Lol", Okay; no more emoji's" ;)

Had I written it myself her response could not have been more perfect. Traveling at the speed of thought my spirit raced to respond getting so excited by the play that my thumb got ahead of my mind and triple clicked the send button before I could stop it.

Left to choose between honest acknowledgement of my excitement and letting what had just happened ride and seeing where it went, I chose to follow my instincts...

Rarely does life, in its day to day form, provide a mind that resonates at a similar speed with a compatible tilt that is capable of such true communication in such a short period of time.

Appreciation for the play drove me to further explain that some of her interaction was unavailable to me due to the technologic inadequacies of the equipment I was using. Emoji's show as [][].

Swirling with intoxication my spirit soared at the beep and leapt skyward upon sight of her, "lol" and further reference to near future interaction!

Inclined as a woman and doubly so inclined as a gay woman, the next seven days were filled with flights of fantastical fantasy.

Could it be, really be, that she knew what I looked like, had spent time interacting with me, had to some degree, I thought, played with me at our first real meeting and then went out of her way to assure there would be future interaction with me?

Each day, I had to recheck all the facts of the case to assure myself I was not building it into something it wasn't.

Of course, like I said, being a woman and gay had to be factored in, not to mention the fact that I'd been shut down, (play wise), for so long that I've been convinced that my interpretive skills, are somewhat askew.

Maybe, she was just responding to the play because it's in the best interest of promoting her meetup site and it really isn't as rare in her life as it has been in mine.

Just one of the many thoughts that kept running through my mind like the loop of sports scores at the bottom of the screen during the "Bloomberg Report."

One of the perks of free will...

I chose to exercise my un-tethered will and stay stoked by my own thoughts...

Regardless of her reasons.

Jethro atmeetupmemoirs

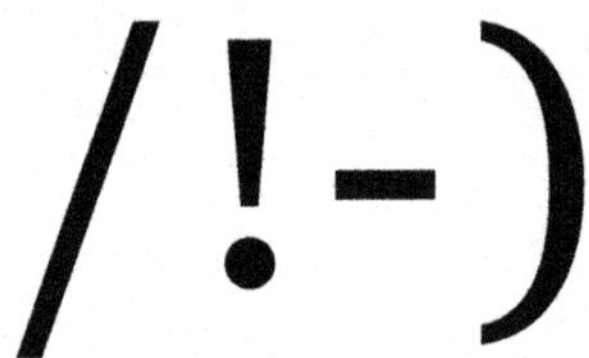

Off the page...

"How long have you been single?", she asked... "if you don't mind me asking?"

Such a simple question, you would think there'd be a simple answer but, of course, there is not...

"Let's see..."

"I've been living alone in my house for about 2 and a half years."

By alone, I mean, with at first, three other souls in the house then there were four and then there were three again...

Inability to guarantee my financial status forced me to choose between my survival and my love for an animal that needed emergency help from doctors that were more interested in the money they could make than keeping our love alive... he paid the price with his life, I paid the price with my soul...

Now there are three, other than me...

Single is a definitive term with a meaning that describes that one is not emotionally, romantically or financially tied to another and is, in all those capacities, available to discover and possibly commit to someone new...

That'll take some breaking down...

2.5 months is all I can claim as far as, believed, emotional availability.

Romantic availability has been some three years or so, from the person I was previously romantically committed to for over thirty years.

Financial, meaning my assets, that are free from encumbrance from any other person, may technically never be true but, for now, for all probable intents and purposes, I'm self- supporting and not supporting anyone else.

Challenged to put all that in a verbal sound bite, I answered, "three years."

My countenance obviously unsettled, she hit me back with an inquiring look and gesture, to further explain.

Unprepared, I gathered my thoughts and stumbled through the break down...

"The woman I spent thirty years with, lives in a separate house on the same property as my house."

"It's a smaller house than the one I live in, behind the main house."

"Like a mother in laws quarters?", she asked.

"Exactly!" I exclaimed, relieved at not having to go into more and more detail.

"Wow, that has to be tough!!", she empathized.

"It's been a complicated and challenging three years that's for sure", I confirmed.

Watching, (I believe), the calculations take place in the mind of our table mate, I ask how long she had been single, to take the focus off me for a minute.

Jethro atmeetupmemoirs

"I just recently stopped on-line dating", she proclaimed, going on to say that she's decided, "it's just not for her."

I responded by acknowledging that, "it seems to be the trend right now, that everybody I've talked to about it has decided it's just not for them" and added my empathetic opinion that, "I would think it's a challenge to try to get to know someone in a three-dimensional way in a two-dimensional environment."

I did not think of it at the time, but it's kind of like trying to get to know a character in a book… never knowing or experiencing that person or their character, off the page…

It's official...

I'm probably going to die old, well without a doubt, it's official that I am going to die, what's not yet, set in stone, is what's going to happen in between now and then and who, if anybody, I'll get to play with during that period.

55 years old now, having lived what I consider to be three or four out of my available, let's say, nine lives… I'm totally unprepared, under qualified and technologically inept for the possible other four or five lives, I may have left.

Realistically, without major schooling in the rapidly disappearing, fine art of getting out of date technology to do updated work, I'm pretty much stuck out in the proverbial cold.

Jethro atmeetupmemoirs

Turns out, to be considered available in this tinder, grinder, match, mingle and meetup world, we live in, you must possess the skills or at least the equipment, necessary to make your intentions known to others via the internet.

Unlike the days of the good old Saturday evening social, where, even someone in my, unique position, (gay, old and gender fluid), had, somewhat of a snowballs chance in hell of dancing up on another old, gay or, at the very least, bi- curious, soul in the same boat...

.	Nowadays, essentially the youth challenged are screwed, simply because without that antiquated, outdated, and usually mercifully, poorly lit, social avenue, the road to re-companioning, is effectively inaccessible.

Pretty much, the whole story about working hard, so you can have the time do nothing all day when you stop working, is a total fallacy as well.

Turns out, the longer you hold still, the more likely it is you'll never be able to get it going again, simply because, if you don't keep it constantly moving, the damn thing, (your body), quits making the oil it needs to keep those, relentlessly aging joints movable and you really do end up stuck, like the Tin man in, "The Wizard of Oz", alone cold and out in the woods, stuck in a body that won't move, with a brain that won't quit.

Don't get me wrong, there are a few things and I do mean, a few things, that are good about being 55.

Such as, you finally legitimately get to enjoy that senior citizens discount at, "Denny's ", you've been illegitimately taking for ten years now.

Unfortunately, you can no longer eat anything they serve...

If you want to live long enough to get your money's worth out of your discount peeriod...

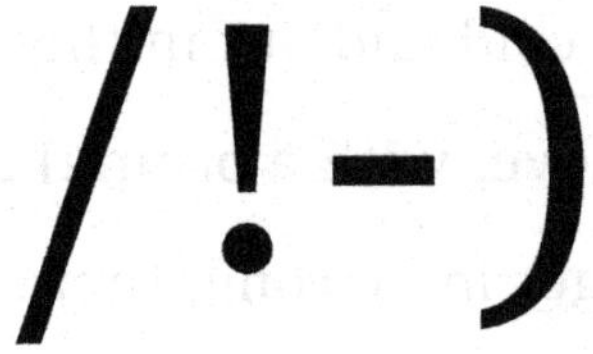

At least twice...

Not nearly as poetic as the "Meetup@Blackrock", Canton title, but at least twice as interesting was the Meetup at Hayden's that made life outside the walls of, "Willow One", seem possible.

20' foot high, medium gray walls, separated, I'm guessing, four different seating sections from what I could see standing at the central hostess podium ten feet inside the door.

Checking in with the hostess, I asked for, "Maggie's group?"

"They're just past the wall on the left", she said and motioned to her right.

Most of the long table at the far left of the room, as I stepped in, already taken, I leaned in and ask the two ladies sitting across from each other at the 10 seat table perpendicular to the long table if the seat at the head of the table, was taken.

"No, not at all go ahead."

"We've got friends coming but there's plenty of room."

Thrilled at my luck at getting the head of the table, I settled in as we introduced our selves and shook hands.

Laura, a medium build blonde, I'd say late thirties, with wavy, lightened hair, was busy consulting her phone and scrolling while talking back and forth with, I think she said her name was Kathy, but I'm not sure.

A three tiered blonde as well, Kathy wore a short layered cut, weighted well at the front and along the occipital and tapered to her nape and was dressed more casually than Laura, in a summer flannel print over a knit shirt.

Thrilled to just observe the goings on, I was caught up in the happenings at the long table making note of the ladies I remembered seeing at the Black Rock.

Meanwhile, the table I was at began to fill with first; a group of four that appeared to have arrived together that took the four spots on the other side of Laura and Kathy.

Moments later, Laura, proclaimed that, "she didn't know where her friends were", adding that, "they were supposed to be here by now", when they came in...

Four of them and only three seats at the table...

Recognition shown in her face as she peeled of her coat and wrapped the chair back to my right with her backpack purse and coat.

Directing her companion to take the seat across from her, they sat as Laura and Kathy announced that, "they weren't eating they were just drinking, so their chairs were not taken... and they'd be at the bar."

Just then a lady... well dressed... who I recognized as the one who was handing out the boxes of Cracker Jack at the Black Rock, stepped up and introduced herself, saying... she didn't think we had met.

"Hi Jeannine", "I'm Sherry", I said, before going on to ask her if she was the organizer and with her acknowledgement, thanking her for, "putting this all together."

North face...

Reverberation along the 14' foot long, high top, granite tabletops, the glass faced wall of the restaurant itself and the dark stained cement floors, caused the cacophony of sound to carry a single voice directly up and out along the corrugated tin roof covering the patio.

Carrying it directly out the 5' foot by 10' foot openings atop the 4' foot cement capped rock wall that ran the length of the 60' foot north face of the Black Rock Bar and Grill.

Ascending with each repeat, we all ended up shouting our names to each other even though we were shaking one another's hand.

Lack of familiarity with the surroundings and each other left us all, I'm sure, feeling somewhat like fifth graders on the first day of school.

Familiar with the concept and basic order of things but unsure how to proceed.

Jethro atmeetupmemoirs

Comfortable that we were all in this together after the initial lull of settling in, mutual eye contact began to require conversation even in its most basic form.

"Where are you from?" she voiced smiling and holding my eyes.

Leaning toward the center of the table, in an attempt to minimize the need to repeat myself or shout, lowering the risk of spitting out the words I voiced, "originally" and before I had finished, she interjected, "I mean now", and I continued with "Westland" and quickly concluded with "Belleville."

Shaking our heads and smiling as a response, rapidly became an acceptable practice to accommodate our inability to converse at a normal decibel level.

Sangria and coffee served to facilitate more and more conversation, giving our minds and spirits the practice necessary to time our speech and the lag time necessary to catch what the other had said without repetition.

Her recent return from a camping trip near Interlochen, brought focus to my attention.

Enchantment over my own recent trip to Interlochen, to see a Melissa Etheridge concert and the addendum to the story that I had been there as a kid competing for state medals as a trumpet player, lead to the announcement of her status as the drummer in an, all girl, rock band, that in the past, had opened for the original, "Kiss ", with, "Gene Simmons."

5'6" inches tall, her full figured, schoolteacher appearance and apparent part time occupation did not read, "rock drummer." Her black, gold and silver, glitter explosion, t-shirt would have been the only clue.

Discussions about the "Tigers", women's basketball, soccer and childhood pass times took us well into the order placing phase of the evening.

Leafed vines decorated the elbows of her partner, recently married over the summer.

Jethro atmeetupmemoirs

Pets, bowling and former Meetup groups she had formed were the topics of conversation with her partner.

Discussion concerning, "Uber", came up as she, (the rock drummer), stated that she drives for them as her main source of income.

My own interest in, "Uber", and the opportunity to get a firsthand, driver review of the occupation, kept me engaged.

Wrapping the conversation with the proclamation that she'd, "have to get someone to do her taxes this year to be able to determine how much she actually made because of all the different incentive programs they have", lead me to volunteer that, "I understood, having driven a semi as an owner operator for ten years and spending $6-700.00 per year to get the business taxes done, not to mention all the highway use taxes and various employment and social security taxes that had to be paid."

Similar features...

They say that it takes a month for every year you're in a relationship to get over it.

Does that mean that for every year you've loved someone it takes a month to stop?

If that is the case, I'm screwed.

I'm looking at 2021 before I can proclaim success in my quest to gct over you.

I'm pretty sure that's way, too long, to wait to begin the process of, "getting a life."

I've managed to not contact you for almost three months now, so I'm guessing that the thought that the problem was, maybe I just didn't give you an opportunity to miss me, doesn't fly.

My real problem is explaining when asked if I'm single that yes... I'm unattached, but not unfettered.

Guess reality is, that, as long as, no one else affects me the way you do, I'm still hooked.

Jethro atmeetupmemoirs

Thought for sure that I'd run into you at one of the meetups I've attended in the last few months but alas, that has not been the case.

Sat on the deck at the first Meetup at Black Rock, Canton and did my best to keep my mind and spirit present while knowing or fantasizing that you were probably exactly five blocks north of me at that very moment.

At one point, I thought I saw you walking across the front of the restaurant talking on the phone, but that woman was at least 25 pounds heavier than you and wearing boots with heels.

Each time I looked away from the women I was having dinner with, the woman I thought was you was walking away, so I'd check back in with my dinner companions for a minute and then check back for you.

Unsuccessful in my quest, the "you", I thought I saw, was gone when I looked back…

.   Moments later I spotted a Landstar trailer being hauled east on Ford.

Landstar being the company I leased my truck and driver services to, I had to smile at the irony.

I'm so adept at making connections that may or may not be there, I'd convinced myself that one of the profiles on the Meetup site named Susan, without any further information available was yours and you were going to be there.

I want to say sad, hey?

Wonder if I'll ever figure it out.

One of the women at the meetup this month could have been your sister if you had one.

Very similar features but 4 inches taller and at least forty pounds heavier.

I'm thinking she thought I was into her based on the number of times she caught me looking at her to convince myself it couldn't be you.

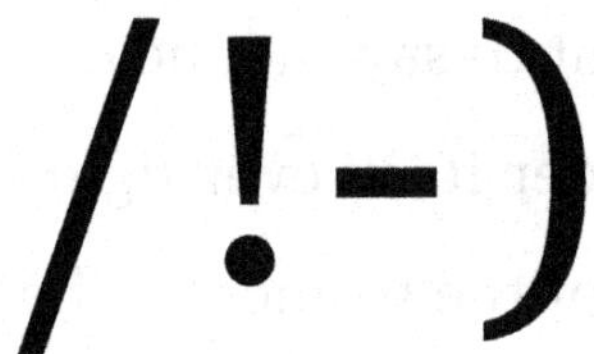

In a nutshell...

You're going to have to swat me on the nose with a rolled-up newspaper.

Obviously, even after all this time and the number of times I've repeated the behavior of trying to or thinking I had gotten over you, I've failed and there are only a few things in my life I have not been able to overcome, apparently, you're one of them.

My name is__________, my problem is____, I'm addicted to________, I've resisted __________for ___days. I have not ____________, in 23 days. I have not __________in 30 days.

I've managed to resist getting a facebook page, ever, figuring it would be just another avenue of rejection.

I'm sure, if I put in the time on the internet, I could find a support group of, "like minded individuals", with, "similar", if not the same, "problem", but I'm not looking for people who have the same problem...

I'm looking for the people who have fixed their problem and grown up and out of it.

Of course, at this point, I'm hanging on, harder than I'm trying to let go... and there it is... in a nutshell.

It's a theme...

Thought you might like to know I found my smile recently!!

Seriously thought I had lost it forever and had no idea, for several years now, where exactly I may have left it.

Have had ideas about how to create a new one and have been working on those ideas for a few years now, which fortunately, has kept me busy enough to allow for the occasional and brief use of the facial muscles involved but nothing that has left those muscles unable to relax...

Interlochen...

Crisply shaded in dappled sunlight filtered through a full summer canopy of old growth trees, enchantment began to fuel my spirit the moment I arrived.

Jethro atmeetupmemoirs

Scaled to human perception, every moment delivered abundant stimuli to each of my senses.

Marked by flags, not more than 50 yards across a courtyard, from where I stood at the one story, round, stone and river rock building that housed the box office, was the venue.

An outdoor amphitheater set into a lakeside hill, bordered by other one story, stone and river rock buildings that housed seemingly endless, knee to eyebrow height windows, all mirroring the greens, golds and deep shadows of the swaying canopy.

Individual 8' by 8' by 8' foot, turquoise canvas awning covered vendor booths ran the length of the pathway with two rows of matching turquoise painted, tubular steel formed picnic tables bustling with those in need of food and drink.

Section 4, row J, seat 6.

Best available, 24' feet out, at eye level, center stage.

Stage south, the setting sun blinded as it descended below the canopy and cast long dark shadows of the trees perpendicular across the central seating area as the final sound checks and stage prep took place.

Able to drop my right hand that held the program shielding me from the sun, a drumbeat, drew my attention to stage left.

Lost in thought, thinking it was yet another sound check, I casually continued my scan left.

One, two and then bam, my brain caught up to what my spirit had already begun to respond to... recognition!!

Out of the shadows Melissa stepped, no fanfare, no announcement, just her and her guitar with each step waiting for the recognition which I and my spirit immediately delivered in the form of the deepest, loudest, most guttural, caterwaul this 55 year old body and soul could produce!!

Held long, strong and pure until she reached center stage, waking up all within the sound of my voice to her arrival...

Jethro atmeetupmemoirs

An acknowledgment smile and nod as she reached center stage, brought about the next even deeper, longer and louder caterwaul inspiring those around me to finally join me in honoring her presence!!

Picking the opening notes to, "No Souvenirs", she waved and gave Hello's to the crowd, who in my opinion, showed not nearly enough excitement even with the schooling they had just received from me, so I gave them another lesson as she leaned back from the microphone... engaged her drummer and bass player to begin the song.

With each signature sway and step to the beat of the music, her shoulder length, undercut, un-face framed blonde hair brushed the top of her sleeveless black leather vest worn above a pair of well-worn blue jeans and black, rounded toe, biker style boots.

Ear to ear the only time my smile relaxed was to reiterate and acknowledge my appreciation for her presence and performance, which I did resoundingly and repeatedly!!

Accustomed to arenas full of enthusiastic women screaming and clambering for her attention, she took everything I offered and at one point announced she wished… she could take me with her everywhere she plays and keep me waiting!!

Obviously, it's a theme!!

Rocked, ever so lovingly out of their slumber, the crowd finally broke out of their repression and began to respond to her offerings with their own whahoowing and affectionately enthusiastic caterwauling, feeding her the fuel she needed to respond in kind with elongated guitar runs and chorus repeats of, "Come to my Window" and "Bring me some Water."

Her cool down chat session, where she gives specific attention to the people of the area, she's in front of gave us insight into the creation of her latest song, written in response to the Orlando night club massacre.

Poignant, "Pulse", carried the crowd through the realization that we're all alive with the pulse of life and love and that love is what keeps all our pulses pounding, no matter who, what or where we are!!

Recognition caused the crowd during the first five notes to break their restraint and fill the isles behind the stage front in the time it took her to sing the first, "Please baby can't you see my mind's a burning hell", of, "I'm the Only One."

All reaching higher to get the best shot on their camera phones she met their needs by playing to the isle fronts for extended periods while the audience and I, in our section remained seated and had better views than all those in the isles at both ends.

Satiated by the prolonged heart pounding rhythmic climax, only she can deliver, we all erupted in thunderous applause voicing our appreciation and appropriately begging for more.

Implication that she intended to exit the stage brought on even more thunder, as she sent away her stagehand bringing out her other guitar telling us that this is where she usually exits and makes us beg for a minute...

Before returning to give us what we want, but tonight, she doesn't have enough time for all that so she's just gonna give us what we want... without all the screaming...

Motioning for her stagehand to bring the guitar back... she approached her microphone stand ... threw back her head... dropped her chin and in her signature hushed tone... seductively... sang...

"Open your back door", launching us all to our feet, singing together... the next line, "I just need to touch you."

All who participated were left out of breath, sweating profusely and hoarse from the highly emotional voicing of her song, "I Want to Come Over" ... while thanking her... for coming over!!

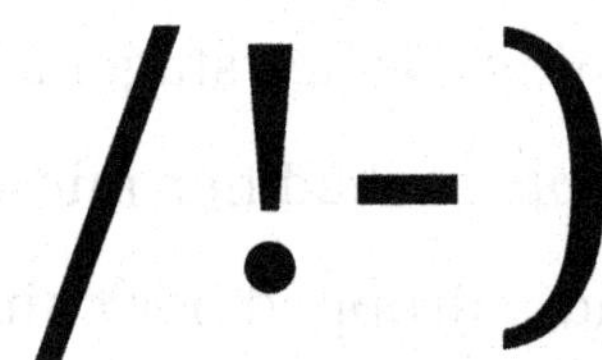

Good press...

Got the whole superhero costume on...

The level of communication and flirtation that had taken place between us during the text exchanges and the Haunted Hayride at Blake's Apple Orchard the next weekend made me think...

Spirits high, I decided since I was already decked out in my street clothes I'd text and see if she wanted to do coffee or a movie with me.

After all, the personal challenge was to go out and meet women who know they like women as opposed to women who just think they'd like to try being with a woman but don't really think they'd like it, yet tell themselves, hey, there must be something to it for all the good press... it gets.

Who's gonna know better... than another woman... how to give a woman what she wants...

Jethro atmeetupmemoirs

Saturday afternoon...

/!-) Got the whole superhero costume on, thought I'd see if you wanna meetup for a coffee or something? /!-)

"Costumes sound fun, what have you been doing?", she messaged back.

/!-) Ran out to Dexter to rendezvous with a statuesque blonde at the truck stop./!-) Text 1.

Thinking that would make it and me sound intriguing...

"Lol, ok..."

"Not sure I know what that means:)"

Thinking you meant you were not sure what the main message had meant I sent the disclaimer message.

/!-)My very married lawyer... /!-) Text 2.

The realization hit me only then, how easily what I'd written could be misconstrued...

Heart beating through my shirt, the seconds turned into minutes and minutes into an eternity with my spirit swirling up and dancing around the living room with each thought that I had done it...

I'd actually... asked her out.

Then with equal, if not more exuberance, the elation that filled my spirit plummeted through the floor like a lead balloon, each time my mind ran a reality check... noting that she hadn't yet responded...

An hour later...

"Going to have to pass on the coffee meetup already got plans to have dinner with a friend."

Hardly able to hold the phone my crushed spirit and I responded...

/!-) Knew it was short notice, /!-) but no guts no glory!! /!-)

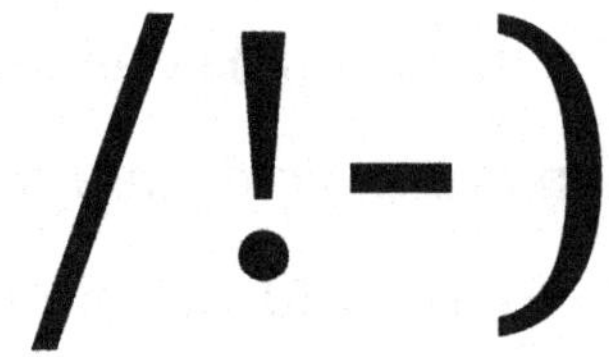

Focus...

Gotta tell ya Grasshopper, there's so much to say and so little opportunity to say it that you'll probably be reading some of it long after I'm gone.

Where do I start?

The longer this interaction goes on the more convinced I am that it was not only serendipitous; it was and is destine.

What do I mean by that, you ask?

I've been wearing a trench in the plywood floor of my bedroom for just over two years.

My goal; to be able to complete my daily activities without chronic pain.

Each step represents a moment in time.

Visualization, a form of attraction according to the experts on such things; is a key to drawing into your life what you are or think you are looking for.

Thoughts slowed down enough to be in the moment during the time it takes each individual muscle involved in executing a step, is a concept I learned from watching, "Kung Fu", when it originally aired in the seventies.

I make minuscule adjustments to my stride, posture and balance... while picturing Keith Carradine, walking through the desert in the sand each time I lose focus and revert to inattentive movement...

Set free...

Captivated by the word play that had started at first text, I had to know if what I thought she may be saying or trying to say was in fact what she was saying or whether my own interpretation was casting shadows on my euphoric spirit.

Elation filled my chest as I read the words...

"I don't use that word casually!"

Set free, my tethered spirit rose and danced about the room swirling up and swooping in ever increasing figure eights while my mind began to imagine some of the many possible future scenarios that may unfold between us.

Large, moisture laden flakes float down and are suspended in time when captured in the cones of soft yellow light along the holiday dressed avenue.

Jethro atmeetupmemoirs

Transcendental, the rhythmic clipity clop, clipity clop, clipity clop of the maple brown Clydesdale's furry blonde hooves echo back at us as we pass by the festive glass paneled store fronts.

Shallow, hardly willing or able to rise in order to take in the cool evening air, my breathing and time slowed as I watched her fingers one by one lift from her thigh, slowly roll and open as she leaned back just enough to slide her hand under my elbow and gently walk her glove covered fingers down the underside of my leather covered arm sending seismic waves of endorphin laden blood up, across, down, through and then back up my spine before rocketing past the back of my neck and out every 1/8 inch long tip of the hairs on the top of my head!!

Folding under the pressure of the adrenaline laden blood being swooshed out of my stomach into my core, I gasp, as she backed her hand out of her glove and slipped her middle finger up and into the v of my rabbit lined leather glove curling her fingers into my palm before wrapping her other gloved hand atop my wrist and turning to pull herself into my grasp.

Immobilized by the rush, time further slowed as she ran her hand from the top of my wrist to the underside of my bicep and lay her head on my shoulder tucking the backside of my arm fully and firmly into the center of her chest...

Caught unaware, I had to will my spirit back into my body from above and just behind, where it had been gliding along on the emotional wave of her embrace when the driver turned to assure our compliance with his request that we exit the carriage to the left minding our step as we disembarked...

Jethro atmeetupmemoirs

54

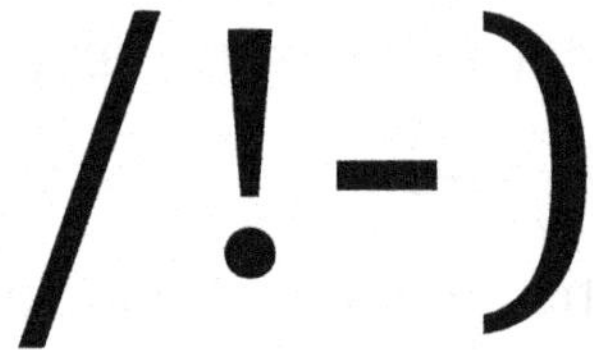

See you soon friend;)...

/!-) Okay, I have to ask, are you trying to let me know that I've been given an honored place in your world or that I've been now and forever placed in the friend zone? /!-)

"I don't use that word casually!"

Here's the deal, as honored as I am and I am honored to be called a "friend", if you knew what the thought of you does to me you wouldn't believe me if I tried to tell you, let alone myself, that I'll be able to accept that compartmentalization.

55 years of life has taught me that life and love only exist in the moment.

Let the moment go and it's gone, you don't get a second chance at it.

Jethro atmeetupmemoirs

Convinced, in the moment that our attraction was mutual, time and our individual psychosis took what was there and transformed it into something else.

It's sad that the influences of society and our need to be accepted by those in our immediate day to day worlds can take such a beautifully natural phenomenon as physical, spiritual and emotional attraction and so effectively kill it.

A solitary entity, love has all the same requirements to stay alive as any other living entity, it just doesn't have a physical presence or manifestation unless put into another vessel such as a child or pet or plant or hobby or passion, etc...

Texts, calling, writing, sending smoke signals, carrier pigeons even hieroglyphics have all historically been employed to... "stoke the flames of passion."

Equally true, I'm sure, it could be said that some of those same technologies have been employed to "extinguish the flames of passion..." as well.

You ride shotgun Susie...

The swirling and sucking started pulling my spirit from above and just ahead of me, down through my body, through my pelvis and out the soles of my leather boots.

Managing to remain upright even though my core had gone limp at the realization of what was about to happen, my instincts had not stopped me from setting myself up for it.

Before the front tires of the van had left the apron of her driveway, the play had begun...

"So", Susie announced, once in the car...

"I'm thrilled to hear you're seeing someone, Julie!"

"How many times have you seen her?"

"Where did you meet?"

Jethro atmeetupmemoirs

"We've met once for coffee and that went well, we've talked on the phone once for an hour", Julie responded.

"I'm glad to hear you say you've talked on the phone!", says Susie.

"We met at a Plymouth meetup a month ago."

"I really like her, she's forty."

"She seems to understand that we live far apart but I'm really anxious to see her again and I really don't want to wait, but I told her I had this event tonight and she seemed to understand."

"I'm kind of glad that she's seen that I have other things going on... it makes it easier to not seem too anxious."

"Yes, you don't want to seem anxious that's a definite turn off!"

"Really want to set up something to see her tomorrow and Monday, while I'm off."

"Thinking I want to text her tonight to arrange it, but I don't know if I should wait until later or do it now."

"What do you think, Sherry?"

"I really like her, I'm really motivated."

How is this possible?

Multiple question marks are slamming hard into my frontal lobe...

Through my head are running these tapes...

Have you gotten your New Year's Eve ticket yet?

At least ten times she'd texted and asked over the two and a half weeks since the Holiday Nights event, that she couldn't attend because of the weather, even though I offered to drive out and pick her up.

If you met this other woman a month ago why not just tell me, you want to go with someone else... why drag me along?

After the dramatic ticketing scenario, where I managed to get the last ticket still available for this evenings, New Year's Celebration, I would think it would have been kinder to just tell me...

Hey, I met someone else I'd rather go with, can we cancel New Year's?

"What do you think Sherry?"

There it is... the fatal blow!

"I don't think I'm the one you should ask for advice about this, Julie."

"This is Van Dyke and 15 Mile", I announced to keep from moving ahead with this line of conversation.

"The g.p.s says it's two and a half miles ahead on the left", Susie replied, adding, "I love G.P.S.!"

"Okay", I said to respond properly.

"I have a really high sex drive, Sherry and if we don't get to see each other this week it'll be another week before we'll get a chance."

"Because of the distance, we can really only see each other once during the week and maybe on the weekends."

"Do you think it's to soon or do you think I should go for it?"

Racing through my mind as I formulate an answer to her latest question is... "What is happening?" ... is she trying to tell me what she wants to happen between us or is this really someone different?"

In an effort not to show my emotional vulnerability I cleared my throat to beef up my voice and said...

"I'm really not knowledgeable enough to advise you on this Julie, I've only been with..."

"Two?", asks Susie...

"Four women in my entire life" I said, "so I'm no expert."

"Usually though one takes the lead", Susie interjects.

"One of the two women usually takes the lead for making things happen, right Sherry?"

"I guess that's true, one is usually dominant."

"I don't mean sexually... although that may be true... I mean as far as in the relationship."

"One person's will... is usually strongest."

"Yes, that's true", Susie agrees and continues...

"Speaking of will..."

"I've decided to cut Pam loose, I've decided she's actually rude and I should just let her go."

"She likes to play games and I'm just not into that!"

"We text back and forth regularly and then... she doesn't respond for three days and is all excited when she does."

"Always excited."

"I mean, really?"

"Who takes... three days... to respond to a text?"

That's a good idea...

"Wonder if that would work for a meetup?"

It's day two, wonder if she's as enamored with the play as I have been?

I managed to not text yesterday or the day before, if the amount of connection between us has been working for her the same way it's been working for me then today should be the day she makes, (hopefully contact with me.)

Get over yourself, she is... twenty years younger than you and has all the technological advancements at her fingertips, she's got plenty of other stimuli other than the miniscule amount you've provided...

Must be the Doctor's office confirming my appointment...

You have 1 unread message.

Click-

Jethro atmeetupmemoirs

"Hey Sherry, don't forget to RSVP for game night on November 19th if you want to go." Emoji emoji.

Okay, stay calm, you asked... and you got the answer, just stay calm...

She is getting something out of it.

She could have just waited to see if I Rsvp'd if her interest was... just as a site organizer.

But you've been... so wrong... before... 45 years' worth... of wrong, so just keep your excitement contained and keep playing it the way you have been and see how she responds.

You know this much... it was her play... and she did!!

Write Message:

/!-) Hey Grasshopper!!," "Have not made it to the library yet this week." "Looking at tomorrow afternoon." "The anticipation is exquisite."

"Was just thinking about you... wondering about a trip to the DIA?"

"Don't know how late they're open though-" /!-)

Send.

Reread.

"Shoot!"

Write message:

Click.

/!-) The anticipation of game night, not the library! /!-)

Send.

Really do need to take the time to reconsider all I've written in the text before I send it... not just reread it for spelling errors.

Okay it's okay, you sent the clarification text if she gets it she'll respond if not...

1 unread message.

"Lol. DIA a definite possibility."

"Any ideas you've got please jot them down or send me an email on Meetup." "I'm looking for more events for after the New Year."

Jethro atmeetupmemoirs

"I'm thinking Greenfield Village Christmas Festival for next month; but that'll get posted later this month." Emoji, emoji, emoji, emoji.

Well, either she gets the double - entendre or she just thinks my honesty at the recognition of the double-entendre is appealing and humorous.

She didn't give me anything to respond to, so I guess that's enough for her for today.

It'll be my play again tomorrow.

November 03, 2016 at 3:11 pm, what are the odds?

Jot them down...

"Jot them down or email me through the meetup site."

Jot them down...

Tracing the edge of your upper lip with the tip of my finger immobilizes you as the wave created from the pressure of my touch ripples along its ridge.

Unable to breathe until the movement ceases, the lack of oxygen heightens the sensations sending a percussive wave down the back of your neck, thundering through your stomach and slamming head long into your...

Pumping ever harder your cardiovascular system instantaneously floods your capillary system with hyper oxygenated blood to plump your skin and heighten sensitivity before they contract to evacuate each

Jethro atmeetupmemoirs

capillary and increase the bloods velocity into all connecting tissue in anticipation of my next touch.

Adrenaline fueled, the blood in my stomach is forced out through the lining making it immediately available to my core in a whoosh...

Locked, my knees begin to quiver as they begin to lose their battle to keep me standing.

My left hand reaches for the edge of the counter behind you as I send my right hand down your left side and lift you onto the edge of the countertop.

Arched and ridged you run your hands up my arms across my shoulders interlace your fingers at the back of my neck and lift your right leg onto my left hip and pull me in.

No longer able to stay locked, my knees buckle with arousal and lean leaving my thighs to counterbalance my dual desire to drive forward and lift and reverse.

Eight inches from heaven...

Using my own words against me...

You'd think I'd learn!!

Close enough to see the swelling of her skin as the blood carried the oxygen to her capillary system that her lungs drew in as she gathered the courage to step over and sit down in front of me.

"What do you do when the object of your attention is a guy?", I asked.

"When it's a guy I let him do all the chasing."

"And because it's a woman... you aren't sure whether you should pursue or lay bait?"

Of course, I didn't get to say all that before her attention was drawn off by the entrance of a couple, we all new from the group that had walked in behind me.

Jethro atmeetupmemoirs

Kisses and hugs all around before it was decided that we should attempt to be seated in the banquet room.

Bringing up the rear is the chivalrous thing to do and my natural inclination, but it does not seem to be serving me well.

Intentionally sitting herself against the wall at the tables end and placing Susie, between us, she happily sat waiting for my reaction to her move.

Choosing not to play, I sat myself on the other side of Susie, where she could hide from my view as she wanted.

Her choice made, I respected it.

Conversation occurred surrounded and dominated by Susie, who showed, (on her phone), and multiple times retold the story of the "Olivia", cruise she had taken this past summer.

Remaining engaged as Susie turned her attention toward me and placated me with the recap, she watched our interaction intently trying to appear un- interested making only glancing eye contact with me as I listened.

Recognizing my opportunity to seek relief I offered my seat to another one of her friends that had just arrived.

"Take my seat, Tammy, I'll be gone for a little while..."

My spirit swirling just ahead and above me is trying desperately to get me to turn my head and look back to see if she's watching but my ego won't let it happen.

All set up, it's clearly the way she wants it.

I just need to get out of her gravity zone and regroup...

In transformation from dinner to dancing, the isle way back to the table was filled with inter table socialization.

Giving me her best, "concerned friend" look, she came to me when she and her friends spotted me... it appeared to be decided that she should come over...

Jethro atmeetupmemoirs

"Are you alright?" "I was worried, I was about to come look for you."

Knowing I would not be able to give her my eyes and honestly answer, I stepped in to speak to the side of her head telling her I was fine before stepping back and briefly meeting her eyes to see if she bought it.

Disbelief showed in her eyes but quickly she gave me a disappointed glance before telling me to follow her back and motioning with her hand.

Not having any other good reason for not wanting to return to the table I said, "there's not anywhere for me to sit over there so I'll just hang here for a while."

Attempt two having failed, I chose to retreat again and regroup after she said, "okay, come over when you're ready", turned and started back to the table.

From the parking lot it all seemed so clear, just walk in and participate.

I've paid my money to be here, there's no reason not to enjoy it.

Back up and tentatively scanning the situation from just above and ahead of me, my spirit dove yet again when having made my way back to the table, those that were sitting, as well as she and her friend Tammy, that I had given my seat to, all jumped up and out of the way offering me any of their chairs.

Touched by their graciousness I tried to decline until one of them turned the chair I had given up toward the dance floor and gestured for me to sit making it undeniable that they had all been discussing me and what I had said before leaving the table about mine being a prime spot to watch the dance floor.

All faces telling me she had told them what I had said and no easily accessible escape, I was forced to take the seat meeting her stare as I sat giving her my direct look of betrayal for her indiscretion.

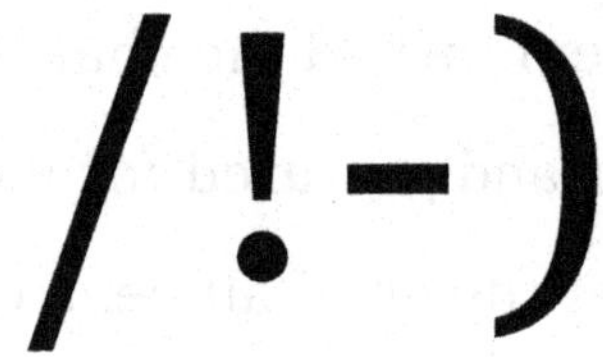

Game night...

"Game night at Julia's has been cancelled we're all meeting at Roger's Roost...", the text read.

Standing at the end of the twelve top table off to the right of the main isle, the look on her face showed what my instincts had been telling me all along...

Taking me in from the tip of my black Lucchessie boots to the top of my Stetson hat, her eyes did not lie, no matter how much her words tried.

Conditioned to misdirect, her insincere hug, designed to discourage any and all display of affection, regardless of attraction, does its job allowing her, intentions test, to continue...

"Sit anywhere you like", she says, directing me past her seat to the same side of the table that appears empty.

"This is, Tammy and Dawn," she says and gestures to indicate each individually.

Jethro atmeetupmemoirs

As I struggle to move my cane to my left hand while pulling off my glove, Tammy sitting directly across from her said, "Hi, nice to meet you", and looked away.

Once out of the glove, I offer my hand to Tammy who is now occupied looking over her shoulder.

Announcing my apologies at the delay I said her name to get her attention took her hand, said my name and offered my pleasure at meeting her.

Dawn, witnessing my struggle took my offered hand, gave me her eyes and said she was happy to meet me.

Stepping around behind her, I assured myself that I hadn't chosen a seat already taken, one away from her seemed like the best bet since there were only five of us here and the site showed that nine had Rsvp'd.

Ear to ear...

Beaming from under the brim of my black banded Granite gray fedora and smiling from ear to ear so proud of herself that she had taken my hat she announced to the room that, "if I ever want to give her a present", she smiled, pointed, tapped the brim and winked...

Recognizing her proclamation as the challenge it was, the room erupted in laughter looking to me and announcing that, I now knew what had to be done...

Through my own laughter I acknowledged the directive but protested that, "it's not anywhere near her birthday yet but I'll keep it in mind."

8' foot long, rough cut farm style tables ran the length of the 40' foot by 20' foot room from the doorway at the long end.

Jethro atmeetupmemoirs

Faux granite faced the fireplace centered with its 36" inch black granite slab hearth, between two window banks on each end.

Directly across from the fireplace, a 48" inch tan granite top bar was lined with ten 2" by 2" ladder style, black, short, backed stools that faced back into the body of the restaurant.

A door at the other end of the room facilitated the flow of wait staff in and out of the atrium.

Five to seven of us made the 5:00p reservation for 25.

Staggered over the next hour or so, late arrivals were announced and introduced around the room until we all sat and filled the end to end tables centered between the bar top and the fireplace.

Conversation ebbed and flowed with minimal lull, due largely, in my opinion, to the fact that everyone had access to new and different people and stories all around.

Our hostess made the rounds joining and commenting on the various topics of conversation as she enlisted some of the staff runners in memorializing the moments of the night for later posting to the meetup site.

Starting out strong the wait staff faded halfway through service dropping the ball by literally disappearing and leaving many of the late arrivals without initial drink and food service.

Comments on the flavors of the brewery offerings were generally favorable.

Our evening together at Roger's Roost two weeks earlier apparently influenced our seating choices.

Gathered at the center of the three, end to end tables, conversation was kept active and amusing as we all took our shots at each other and our jointly recognized… "behavioral patterns."

Jethro atmeetupmemoirs

Just as it had begun, the evening waned with the trickled departure of couples first... then the singles began to announce their different animals that needed tending, until just the seven from Roger's Roost were left at just after seven in the evening in need of additional excitement and or a different venue.

Drawn in from so many remote areas, no central location known to all with the possible entertainment capabilities we were all interested in was known to be in the immediate area.

Sheer will, brought about a suggestion from the most experienced among us and we all loaded up and moved the party south to, "Scooter's", on Woodward and 9 Mile.

Infamous for their shower curtained "female facilities..." we all settled in against the back wall at some wobbly brown, Formica wrapped, dive bar tables and chairs thinking, I'm sure, that the evening was going to bring wall to wall lesbian sighting possibilities.

Wider brimmed, her black fedora out shinned mine as she leaned into the group allowing ample time for appreciation of her well - presented white button down, open to the fourth button, big tip generating shirt as she took orders for beers all around.

Surprise and respect shown on her face at the coffee with cream order I placed.

Bringing up the rear as we entered, left me facing the brick wall with my back to the room and at the opposite end from our hostess.

Atmospheric change slowed the joy and frivolity to a crawl as the room behind us filled with mostly straight couples there to drink and wait for karaoke to begin.

"Glen Miller" and "Benny Goodman" from the juke box provided the background to the slow revival of the group to pre arrival excitement levels.

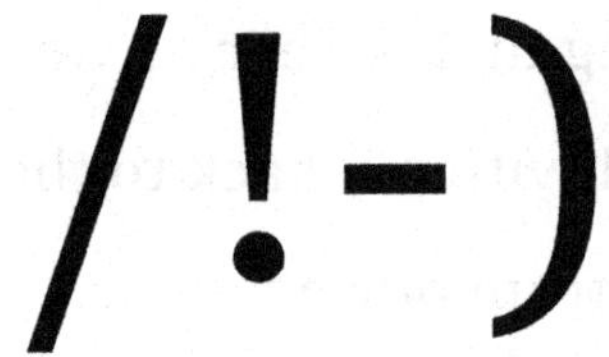

Entertained...

/!-) Hey Grasshopper, Thanks for yet another evening filled with beautiful, lively women and spirited fun! /!-)

1 unread message:

Click-

"Thanks for coming last night Sherry; look forward to future events... I'm glad you were entertained:)"

/!-) I was, but let me be clear... I enjoyed the attention I got from you the most and look forward to future opportunities to play! /!-)

"Lol! You are a writer:)"

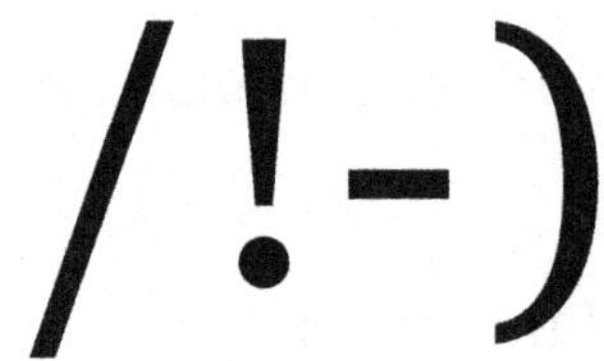

So wrong...

"I've been so wrong before!"

"What?" I asked.

"I said women suck!" She repeated.

"They do?" I asked. "Are they good at it?"

The look on her face when she leaned back and told me that she wasn't kidding, meant I had to lean in and ask what she was talking about.

"Women, they suck", she repeated, giving me her eyes.

"Okay, you're going to have to be more..." I started to say...

Not able to hear me over the karaoke being caterwauled from the stage she turned and brought her head closer to my lips...

Rendered unable to speak, seconds slowed to minutes as my mind blanked and my spirit drank in as much of her energy as possible while waiting for my brain to catch up and execute the orders given by my spirit to...

Further slowing time her hand atop my coat that lay doubled over my thigh to keep it off the floor had my mind busy trying to absorb her touch through the leather and jeans between me and it.

Sheer willpower brought my spirit back from it's whirl up and around our bodies at an ever increasing pace releasing the hold on my biologic function and allowing for the deep draw of oxygen necessary for movement of the blood back to my brain.

Once able to execute on the orders being repeatedly sent from my spirit to my brain to, speak, I managed to choke out...

"I'm sure it's not you, I mean, I don't know enough to say what it is but I'm sure whatever the problem is that it's not you" before she could think I'm just an idiot and not so totally paralyzed by excitement and my proximity to her that I've lost all connection with my brain!

A picture...

Now that I replay it... the parallels are stunning.

Door to the basement just off the dining room...

The dog is smaller and a different breed and there is a cat that there was not in her house but the rushes and flushes from the emotional roller coaster were very much the same.

Funny no matter what our age, (so far that is), the rapid escalation emotion takes through our bodies does not lessen like the sensitivity of our skin to detect touch or our noses to filter scent from the air...

Emotionally I think our wiring turns the minor aggravation emotions to anger and the inspirational emotions to tears leaving us with only the most basic of emotions with which to function.

In reality... we may function better without them but what would be our reason to keep fighting the good fight without the quest for one more good rush of emotion?

In the current instance, she left the room to greet her "friend", (Susie), when her father opened the basement door and tossed a toy down the stairs, sending me into the sucking, swirling, spinning and distortion of time and space that comes with the onset of de ja vu.

Drawn down from above and about five feet in front of me my spirit reentered my body about the same time the hormonal rush hit my stomach making it feel as if the floor had dropped away from under my feet and I found myself struggling to stay on the edge of the stool...

"I want to get a picture of us", she said as she reentered the room from greeting Susie...

"Can you take a picture of us", she asked as she stepped toward me and handed me her smart phone.

Sick with dread from the de ja vu, I was hardly able to physically respond to her request but powered through and took the phone from her when she reached me.

"Now what?" I asked.

"I'm sorry", I said, "but I have absolutely no idea how to take a picture with this.

"I don't have one and have no experience with how to work one", fumbling to hold on to and not drop it.

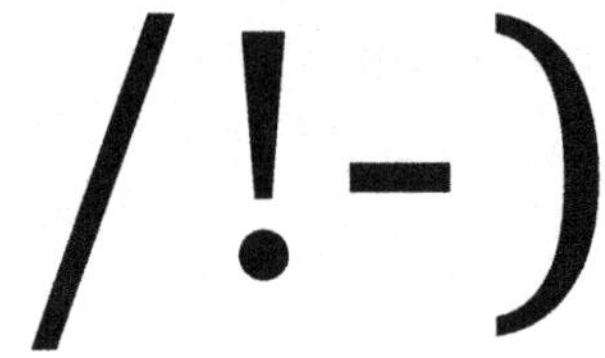

Seven seconds...

"ZaZa no... ZaZa... No ZaZa... ZaZa come, ZaZa, down, ZaZa come on, ZaZa down", her voice rang out from the other side of the door, commanding their black standard poodle come down from the top of the basement stairs, where she, (ZaZa), was doing her best to protect her territory from whom ever it was that, seemed to her, to be crazy enough to be giggling the handle.

With the first vibration of her voice in my ear, my vision narrowed, the blood drained from my head, flooded my ears, deafening me, on its way to my lungs, where it quickly dried my mouth, before shortening my breath to a gasp, all in the time it took for her to climb the stairs, twist the thumb latch and pull ZaZa back down the stairs.

Realizing ZaZa had stopped barking, something told me to try the handle again, it began to turn, I felt the latch spring free and my spirit soar, I was about to get to see her, for the first time since my brother's wedding.

Stepping through the doorway, I heard her older brother say, "What do you think your little girlfriend would think if she knew what we just did?"

Eight full heart beats and four short breaths is exactly how many contractions took place, how much oxygen was converted to carbon dioxide while the various different and distinct sound waves generated by his mouth and tongue, traveled in waves and were captured in my ears and deciphered by my brain.

Instantaneously re-coded into a chemical signal, those sound waves, traveled thirty seven miles along my central nervous system, shot through my heart valve and pierced my hearts protective membrane, before unleashing the deadly chemical endorphin package, specifically formulated, to stop its function.

Now rendered physically seized and emotionally shattered, my heart dropped so hard, I was hardly able to keep my knees under me and stop myself from falling forward, down the stairs, as my spirit crashed.

ZaZa, now aware of my presence, pulled away and bolted up the stairs, ducking around my legs and dashing through the door, still open with the handle still in my hand, behind me.

The way she turned away when our eyes met and she realized I probably heard what he had said, told me all I needed to know...

Stunned, I stood at the top of the stairs waiting for my stomach to rejoin my body, from the floor where it found itself, the moment our eyes met.

ZaZa, then blasted past me and bounded down the stairs.

Jethro atmeetupmemoirs

At the bottom, her brother, in a show of dominance, took ZaZa by the collar and put her in a room behind the bar.

Just as the yanking of the handle had brought my body and spirit back together, the slamming of the door, sent it flying down the stairs, desperately, in search of any kind of sign, that what had just happened, was all, a bad dream and not the first seven seconds of what was supposed to be, at least in my mind, a weekend in heaven with the one person, in the world, I thought for sure, loved me.

Smile if you love me...

Five words.

One picture.

Captured.

Undeniable.

Proof.

A moment in time... click

'84 in block letters on a mug on the top shelf of the flat, country blue plate rack marks the year.

At a dark, round kitchen table, set with matching country blue and white gingham checked, oval shaped and fringed, place mats.

Participants all sitting in simple ladder backed, country blue chairs as if in a scene from a tv show where

Jethro atmeetupmemoirs

the camera, literally, is the fifth, or sixth, person in this case.

Six placemats, two ashtrays, one cup of coffee and a highball glass with a single, twenty minutes melted, cube, floating in the Vernor's that tickled my nose when I took that first, effervescent drink.

Adrenaline charged, oxygen swollen blood races through my veins, at the speed of thought, putting my legs in motion, lifting me to my feet and the camera up to my eye, in one smooth motion, giving my body time to catch up with the plan my subconscious had chemically delivered, upon the birth, of that infamously speedy, thought...

"Here it is, this is your chance, my spirit screams, your chance to get the truth, (because a picture is worth a thousand words and pictures don't lie), if you don't smile, I'll know, my sister, (the one, looking away in the picture), was right. If you do smile, I'll know reality and have proof of it, for life!!"

Say it, what have you got to lose?

Milliseconds tick away as my breathing deepens in anticipation of speech... laughter erupts as the recognition of what I had said, instead of cheese, hits them.

Milliseconds, slow to billiseconds as through the camera eye, I watch your smile break and spread, lifting your brow and tilting back your head as your laughter lights up your eyes and your smile continues to spread and widen.

Recognition faster than acknowledgement triggers the endorphin release that is rapidly disabling my ability to stand, I have to act fast.

Push the button, my spirit screams inside my head, push the button now, you have to push the button, push the button, tick, tick, tick, tick... ccccclllliiiiiccccckkkk.

Side by side, closer to each other than anyone else in the room, our mothers, together, your mom's left arm extended in what, a psychologist would say, is a protective position, her right hand tucked under the thigh of her crossed leg.

Jethro atmeetupmemoirs

Fully covered, neck to wrist, in her signature pull over pink sweater, pulled over, her full collared, button down shirt, blue docker style pants and I'm guessing, because the picture doesn't show, black, soft leather, lace up shoes and white sox.

Shoulder to shoulder, arm against arm, their undeniable love and unwavering friendship, has kept them within five miles of each other throughout some, 45 years and two different states.

A Similar state...

The exact wording escapes me... and it was so long ago the text has been deleted off my phone but the jest of it was that you were either in need of or looking forward to a good night out and hoped that we could do it soon...

You know me well enough to know the way I'm going to interpret what you've said... and you so often drop off the map... that most of the time the words you've left me with are all I have to work with.

There was also talk before this last communication black out that we were going to have to form our own Meetup group.

I'm guessing that was about playing cards, but that's just a guess.

Forming our own Meetup group would be pointless if the reason is to find someone to have a relationship with.

Jethro atmeetupmemoirs

There are not enough days left in this lifetime to develop a real relationship.

Most of the Meetups that I've encountered only meet once or twice a month and when they take place everyone is so busy working through their own psychosis and fears they seem to either be in a fog or so paranoid about what you may be after that filtering through it all would take years.

I think I've discovered that I really don't want a relationship, at least not in the sense that my time and energy is devoted to the happiness of another.

I'm pretty sure that I don't want anybody else's time and energy devoted to my happiness either.

Specifically, I want to play and have fun with someone who wants to play and have fun too. Someone who is in a similar state of life having worked a lifetime to get what they have and knows themselves well enough to know how they want to spend their available time and resources without having to be convinced.

If we're talking love, we're talking someone who's willing and able to tell and show me that she's not intimidated by the world or me.

That may prove to be harder to find or achieve than any of the other challenges I've taken on, but I've got nothing but time.

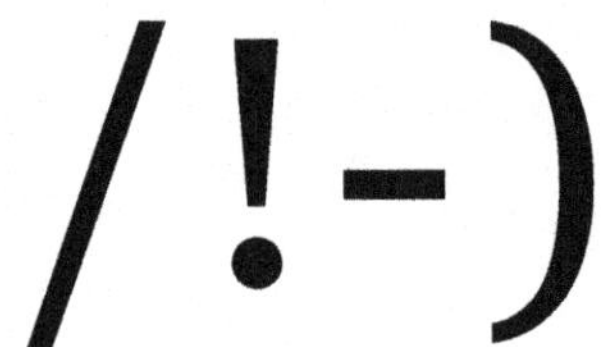

As I am...

Ok, I get that you don't want to, "date me", but I wouldn't tell you that I'm not attracted to you to spend time with you when I was eight and I won't do it now.

So, I guess, just like then, what I need is to let you know that if you want to spend time with me as I am, a woman, attracted to women that because you are a woman, you're in my potential dating pool.

For the most part, I get that it's reasonable that you'd have to treat me like any man who's shown an interest in you, because of the probable encouragement factor.

/!-)

Highly suggestible...

Everything from one ringy dingy, two ringy dingy, to my name is Edith Ann and that's the truth, followed by a long tongue wagging, lip vibrating, spit slinging display of childish affect made famous by, Lily Tomlin.

Back when you and I were both of an age to think it was funny and are still now of an age capable of remembering when it was on," Laugh In", has run through my mind in the last week.

Problem: How the hell do I illustrate the tongue wagging in a text, or do I call your phone and leave you the one ringy dingy, two ringy dingy, message and hope you get the reference?

Did you know that Lily Tomlin, is and always has been gay?

Jethro atmeetupmemoirs

I didn't find out about her being gay until, I'd say the year 2000 or so and I just heard her say the other day on, "The Late, Late, show with James Corden", that she and her partner have been together for over 45 years.

I'm thinking the explanation for the whole, "Mrs. Beasley ", doll phenomenon that occurred over Christmas, 1969, had something to do with Edith Ann and the whole, "and that's the truth", bit.

When she, (Lily Tomlin), did that character, she always held that doll in her arms while she rocked in that oversized rocking chair and that somehow made me think I wanted a doll.

Of course, the "Mrs. Beasley ", doll itself, came from, "Family Affair", which was another of the five or so shows that regularly saturated my highly suggestible, childhood mind.

Who knows?

We've all been influenced by the medium.

In fact, I was talking to your mom and one of her fellow residents the other day, who out of the blue ask me if I was a dog lover.

Strange, but then...

Her question, brought to mind, ZaZa, so I turned and ask your mom if she ever replaced ZaZa.

I could tell by her reaction to the question that it had been quite a while since anyone had spoken to her about, ZaZa.

She was clearly surprised I remembered her.

If memory serves, ZaZa, was named after ZaZa Gabor, wasn't she?

The connection still clearly eludes me.

After all, ZaZa Gabor was a platinum blonde and ZaZa the dog, was a Standard Black poodle.

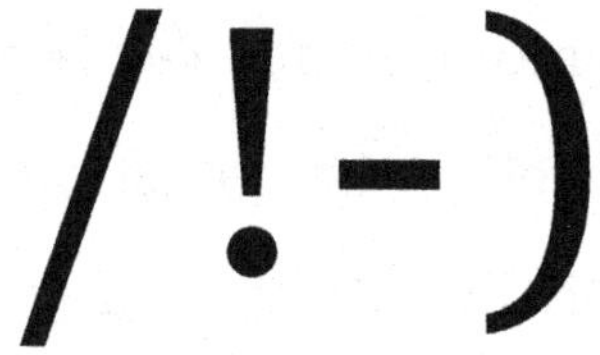

Somewhere out there...

Tuesday: October 13, 2015   12:56 a.m.

To: Elusive @ First Class Mail

From: Illusional @ Somewhere Out There

I'm going to use this format to communicate with you in the present.

I'm currently writing you the story of what happened when I got to see your mom for the week and a half before she was, so I was told, no longer in residence.

I've been working on finding my writing voice for about nine months now.

I got a book from the library about how to write your first novel in 6 months as a possible means of expressing my angst, in all its forms.

Of course, it's now... nine months and what I've got is a folder full of work that wouldn't by any stretch of the imagination (and believe me, I express some imagination), be called a book.

Jethro atmeetupmemoirs

However, in writing you the letter about your mom, I discovered I'm able to just write from experience and speak from my thoughts, at least, while speaking / writing to you.

I think it's always been that way for me.

The way I remember it, I got us in trouble for keeping, you, on the phone for over 200 minutes way back when, what was it 1969 / 70?

They had just started charging a toll for calls made in the same area code. (Which is what got us caught, by the way.)

Your Mom noticed the 200 minute call noted on her bill and called my mom to find out if it was an error.

I'm pretty sure the last thing you said to me during our 88 minute marathon conversation in August 2015, just before my phone cut out, was, that, you didn't have to get up in the morning, in response to me saying, "I should go, if I'm keeping you up and you have to work in the morning."

Thought a fool...

Keep wanting to write you love letters...

Keep wanting to send you the ones I've already written...

My father always said, "it's better to be thought a fool... than open your mouth and confirm it."

I just wrote 20 pages, at least, in response and about my response to a woman who reacted to me and my energy just exactly as I would have ordered it, had I custom ordered it.

Yet those pages sit here printed out, addressed, with a cover letter, on my desk, un-mailed for fear that they may be misunderstood.

I'm so capable of romanticizing and have been so ridiculed for so long for doing just that, that I've forgotten how to just act and react without the fear.

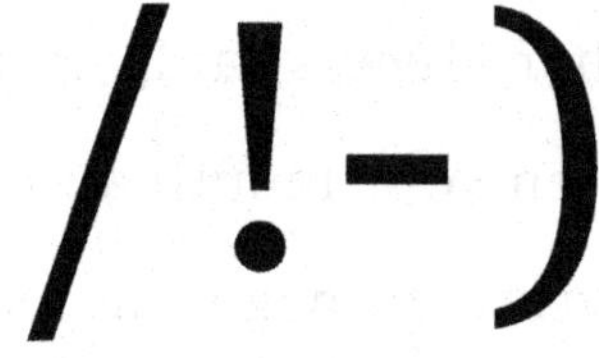

Better sell...

Personal happiness seeking trends require us to better sell ourselves to achieve the hookup we think, we are looking for, but reality doesn't work like that.

Reality is, the way the universe works is just the opposite.

Through our thoughts, dreams and desires we tell the universe what we think we want and keep refining those requests until before us, stands the very thing we've been asking for.

Then our job is to recognize what we're seeing and seize it.

As opposed to applying for the job, we are interviewing and posting the job listing and waiting for the applicant to arrive.

Jethro atmeetupmemoirs

Our conditioning as Americans, especially female Americans is to believe we are applicants as opposed to employers.

Between every two people regardless of gender there is only one contract that can be negotiated.

Employer employee.

That is not to say that each one does not act in both capacities within the relationship.

In fact, the ultimate mutually beneficial contract would require each entity to perform in each capacity in specific ways recognized and agreed upon by both.

Oh boy goodie...

When I turn off all the lights and the only sounds are the radio playing in the other room and the splash of tires as the 18 wheels of the trucks roll by outside the windows of my house, I find myself thinking about you, picturing your face next to me at Hayden's in Canton the second time we saw each other, the first time we met.

The look on your face when I told you I was a writer...

You literally clapped your hands in front of your, "Oh boy goodie... face!"

Captured in that moment I watched as your pupils swelled like the shutter of a camera lens seeking to let in all available light.

You drank me in as if I had manifest in that moment, right before your very eyes.

You'd been waiting for me...

Jethro atmeetupmemoirs

The greenish gray of the walls around us faded to black, I swear I could hear the whoosh of the air as you drew your next breath and feel the movement of warm air through the hair on the back of my right hand at rest on the white cotton tablecloth as you turned toward me gave me your eyes and were finally able to relax and release that same breath...

"Really?" You ask...

"Well, an aspiring writer", I qualified my proclamation by owning that I had not had anything published yet.

"Julie's written three books", said your friend that had taken the seat opposite you and directly to my left.

Making it my turn to return the, "really?" and re-engage your eyes...

"Yes, they're all available on Amazon", you said, holding my gaze.

"This is Sam, by the way", gesturing your introduction with your right hand as I took in the image

/ message on the front of your black t-shirt before checking back in and acknowledging what had been said by turning to Sam and offering my hand…

"I'm Sherry, it's nice to meet you Sam", I said while scanning her countenance for signs of discomfort over our prolonged exchange.

No reaction visible, I went on to ask Sam what she did for a living taking in her short cut, auburn hair, light brown, slightly gold eyes and fair, freckled skin while she sat arms crossed looking like she's frozen in her short brown, Carhartt, winter jacket, tan stand up collared sweater over an orange t-shirt.

"I work in housekeeping at a senior living facility right now but I'm about to go back to school, I had signed up to go to, ITT Tech, just before they shut down, so I had to change my plan and decided to go in another direction."

"Yes, I was in the process of getting or trying to get a job with them when all that happened", you said…

Drawing the conversation back to you.

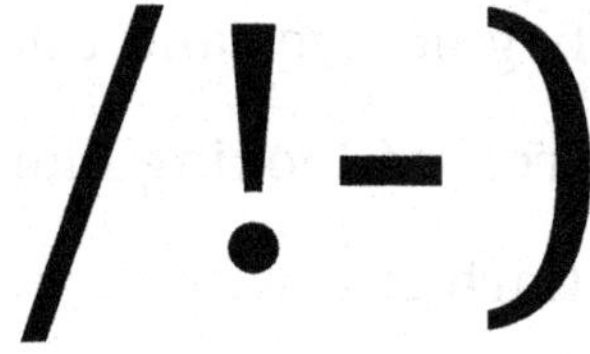

Tidal wave...

"The Grasshopper Irish Pub", somewhere in, New Jersey, was featured on, "What Would You Do?", on, "Abc", tonight..." "Planet Fitness", was the scene of two men, thought to be on fire, when they entered the "Planet Fitness", at the corner of Van Dyke and 23 mile, in Shelby Township, tonight...

Kinda hard to keep you off my mind when it seems the universe keeps sending up smoke signals...

Not that I was having much success at otherwise occupying my mind...

Mostly I'd been repeatedly pondering what might happen if I just, "put down into words...", yet another connection, "Elton John", was featured prominently on the "20/20" episode about, "Versace's Murder."

Sometimes there is just no escaping one's own mind... or the t.v. it seems...

Jethro atmeetupmemoirs

Truly wish it was as simple, as hitting the off button sometimes!!

But then again, the fact that I can think anything I want, anytime I want, is kinda cool.

Technically, I can even write down anything I think, anytime I think it and there really isn't any rule that exists that can stop me.

Again, very cool and truly American.

So, anyway, I was wondering earlier, if I actually wrote down and emailed to you what I'd like to do with and to you, whether it'd be more or less likely that I'd ever get to do any of it?

Guess there's only one way to find out…

Ready??

Has your breathing gone shallow??

Can you feel the slamming of your upper heart valve in your chest as it struggles to accommodate the increased volume of adrenaline laced blood flooding into your heart, swelling and stretching each chamber wall before…

At capacity, the walls in unison urgently constrict to… keep from bursting, forcing the lower chamber valve to slam open creating that signature tidal wave, whoosh, of blood moving at a hyper accelerated velocity, toward your stomach?

Grasshopper?

/!-)

Lost in thought...

Me too! ;)

Day dreamin.

I wanna do... things to you...

My friend who emphatically told me just two weeks ago on the phone that you were "not", too young for me, is, now that the New Year is over, telling me that you, "are" to young for me.

You light up when I come into the room and whether you realize it or not you never really take your eyes off me.

Unless I've been locked in a cave for the last thirty years, (which is a real probability), that's attraction, in its most simple form.

Our eyes seek out what we want.

Jethro atmeetupmemoirs

It would not be fair to you.

I've lived a whole lifetime since I was your age… you would always be a lifetime behind.

I can offer no upgrade of your present situation.

If all those reasons are not, enough I've got at least ten more that I really don't want to write down but they're real, nonetheless.

Unfortunately for me that does not stop or has not stopped me from…

Getting lost in the thought of my lips against your neck as I pull you into my arms and slowly lift you high enough to wrap your legs around my waist and spin to turn us out of any doorway in which we meet.

Chutes and Ladders...

/!-) Grasshopper,

Chess is a game of strategy that has challenged kings and brought down empires, but it's the equivalent to, "Chutes and Ladders", compared to a good game of attraction.

Similar to chess, each move has and creates hundreds of possible outcomes that are then changed and either increased or decreased in relevance by the previous move.

Subsequently, like thermal nuclear war, a game of attraction cannot produce a winner, once begun.

A winner can only be established prior to the game.

/!-) Shakespear! /!-)

Jethro atmeetupmemoirs

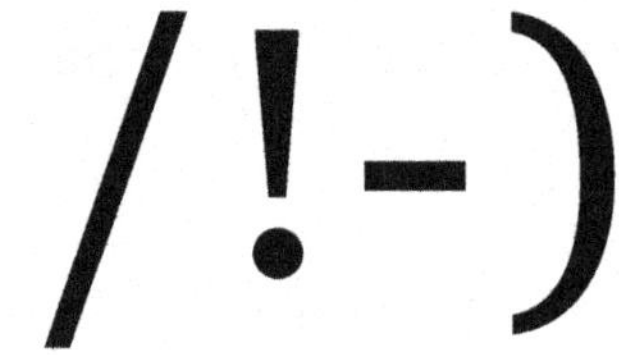

Above and beyond...

Rate this Meetup:

M.G.L. / Pride 2017 brought to those in attendance all the sights, sounds, entertainment and atmosphere the purpose and the people it honors could deliver!!

Bright blue skies... 86 degrees... a cool breeze off the Detroit River and the corner of Woodward and Jefferson crowd steadily grew as the people of the Motor City displayed their colors and showed their support through all forms of banners, flags, bobbles and beads.

Provided with smooth processing through the gates the crowds appeared to be cheerful in anticipation of the afternoon events.

Michigan's most abundant resource proved vital in keeping the crowds comfortable throughout the afternoon.

Ice cold bottled water was available for hydration while a full 360 degrees of cascading water from the fountain brought cooling relief from the heat to those in need.

Above and beyond, once again, the members of Metro Gay Ladies played, paid close attention to and brought smiles to each other's faces.

Hats off to M.G.L. and "Motor City Pride", for making another glorious afternoon in the company of "family" and "friends", possible!! /!-)

Mesmerized...

Can I help?

My inner dialogue had my frontal lobe tied up with the happiness hormones flooding the area from having made it through the gates and onto, "Hart Plaza" after the "Pride Parade."

Freedom and I had made it in as planned.

My elation at achieving that alone was enough to distract me from the fact that all the other Metro Gay Ladies had left the area and you were standing in front of me alone with two bottles of water.

One on the table next to you that was frosted with condensation and the other in your right hand and only a third full.

I noticed you look left toward me as I rode up...

In one smooth motion you twisted off the cap of the one third full bottle, reached up and back to gather the hair at the nape of your neck, breathe in and bend forward at the waist, (I assume to allow the water you were about to pour over your neck to fall clear of your shoulders), look left, (again I assume to verify my position), announce that you were going to pour the water on your head to cool off... before you started to pour...

Pupils dilating, my peripheral vision reduced so fast all I was able to do was apply the brake as the adrenaline was being sprayed into the chemical hormone bath that was flooding my brain as it passed through my pituitary gland on its way to my central nervous system that had already shut down all cognitive function at the first moment of realization of what was taking place in front of me!

My spirit, a full 3 seconds ahead of my cognitive function was already in the process of prepping my approach to allow me to step quickly off Freedom, take the bottle from your hand while you were still bent over and drizzle it languidly over the back of your neck while your central nervous system thrilled at the cool water flowing down the back of your neck along your jaw line and off the end of your chin...

Meanwhile, because of the cognitive shut down and subsequent freezing of all other life sustaining functions, I was forced to wait for the chemically coded blood to arrive at each organ in turn rendering me unable to take in the oxygen needed to move the muscles involved in the formation of words...

Once able to move from my frozen state, it was too late... you had already lifted from your bent position and (I'm assuming), decided you had accomplished the two tasks you'd set out to do and were already moving on from the moment before I got out the words... but... mesmerized by your play... I did not lose focus and was able to watch your smile break wide at the sound of my voice cracking as I ask...

"Can I help?"

Jethro atmeetupmemoirs

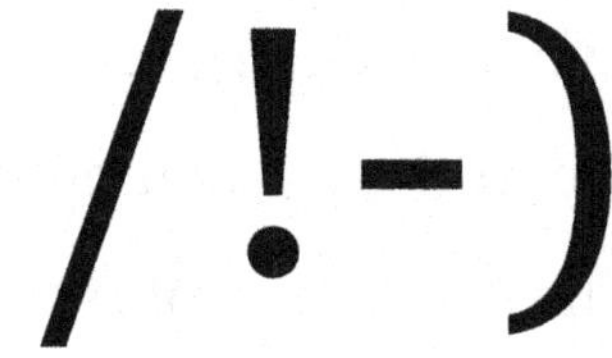

Soon...

1 unread message:

Click-

"Very well written Sherry;) I hope one of your books is published soon!"

Write Message:

Click-

/!-) Thanks Grasshopper! Me too! Working the process! /!-)

©2017/!-)Sherry Craven/!-)Jethro

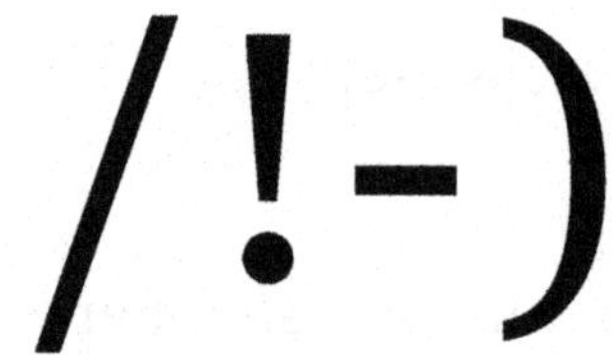

Acknowledgements

/!-) Grasshopper,

The writer writes the story the artist expresses

through paint, while the musician makes audible the

emotions the poets, words portray. /!-)

Thanks for the game!

Shakespear! /!-)

/!-) Jeannine,

Thank you for always making me feel welcome at your

Meetups!!!

Sherry /!-)

/!-) Melissa,

Thank You 4 Always resonating Truth, giving Voice to

our Spirits, stimulating our Minds, rocking our Bodies

and soothing our Souls. /!-)

/!-)

Back cover photo of Author courtesy of:

Fran!

Thank you, Fran, for taking one of the only good photos

of me in existence!

/!-)

meetupSeriesmemoirs

Fb... beyond Meetup@Blackrock

"It's a post me, tag me, swipe me right world!"

next2u@Meetup@Blackrock

"If I sit... I'll want... If I... I'll want more!"

****

exquisiteEncountersseries

High Blood Pressure

a tangible manifestation...

****

motorCitymemoirs

Of... Breach of Trust

law, love, life...

****

Lilley Ford

a little story...

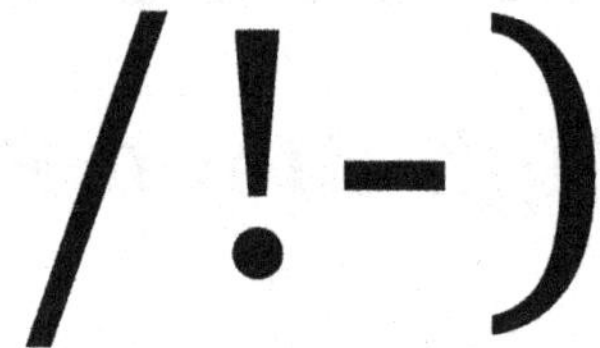

Dear Reader,

There are only so many questions a writer needs answered by their readers to know if what they have written is worthy... of the readers time.

Did the first sentence make you want to read the second?

Did the first page flow and cause you to want to read the second page?

How many minutes did you read before you thought to yourself where is this going?

How many times did you have to reread what you'd already read to pick up on something you missed or wasn't available for clarification?

Did the writing draw you into the scene/circumstance/moment?

Did you find yourself making connections that were not necessarily clearly stated within the lines on the page?

Did you recall previously read information between sessions of reading?

Jethro atmeetupmemoirs

Did you find yourself thinking about what you had read when away from the story and wondering what might happen next?

Were you able to accurately anticipate what might happen next?

Were you and your beliefs reflected, to any degree, in one or more of the characters?

Did you read more than the first three pages in your first session?

Did the synopsis make you feel as if you had foreknowledge once engaged in the story?

Did you have ah-ha, moments?

Moments when previously given details or story line suddenly had expanded or new meaning that was not previously clear?

How often did you have to search a paragraph to find your place after an interruption, loss of place or waning of interest?

I know I said there were only so many questions...

As writer's we don't get a chance to receive spontaneous feedback until our work is turned into a play, a movie or if we're lucky... a Netflix endeavor... but I'm confident they, Netflix, only look at the works of writers lucky enough to have received reviews from the readers...

Make my day...

Scan or take a picture of the QR Code below with your smart phone and from a computer... publish your review.

Hope you enjoyed the read!!

/!-)

Made in the USA
Monee, IL
07 July 2026